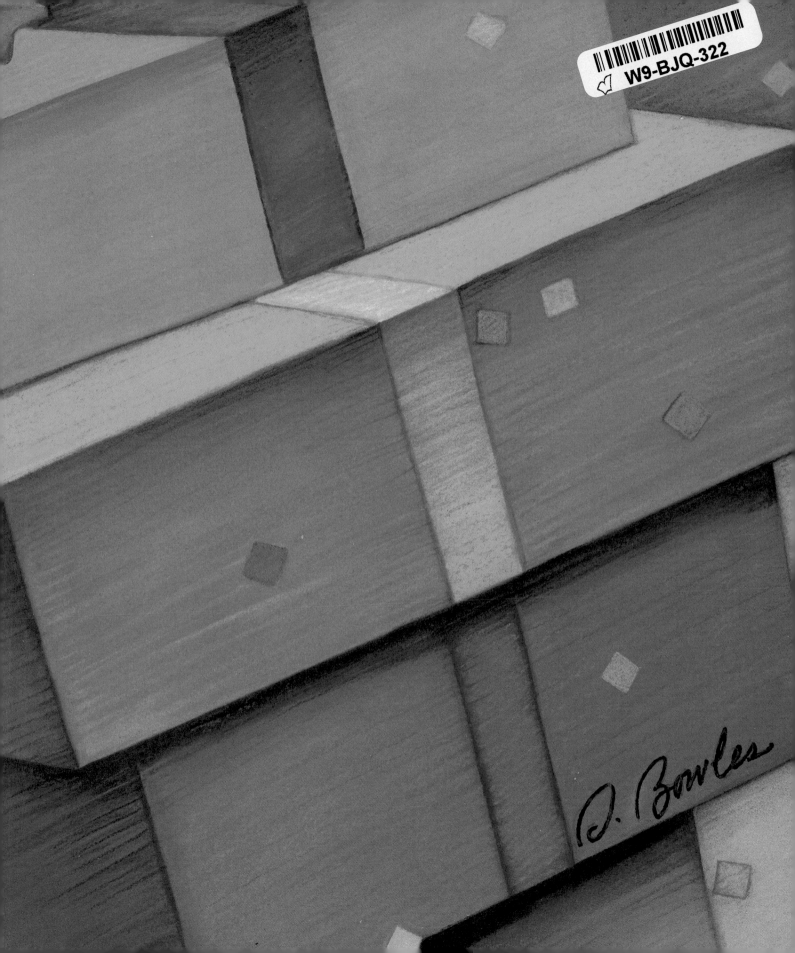

J. Bowles

Big Dreams

Senior Authors

Roger C. Farr

Dorothy S. Strickland

Authors

Richard F. Abrahamson ♦ Alma Flor Ada ♦ Barbara Bowen Coulter
Bernice E. Cullinan ♦ Margaret A. Gallego
W. Dorsey Hammond
Nancy Roser ♦ Junko Yokota ♦ Hallie Kay Yopp

Senior Consultant

Asa G. Hilliard III

Consultants

Lee Bennett Hopkins ♦ Stephen Krashen ♦ David A. Monti ♦ Rosalia Salinas

H A R C O U R T   B R A C E   &   C o m p a n y

Orlando Atlanta Austin Boston San Francisco Chicago Dallas New York Toronto London

Requests for permission to make copies of any part of the work should be mailed to: School Permissions, Harcourt Brace & Company, 6277 Sea Harbor Drive, Orlando, Florida 32887-6777.

HARCOURT BRACE and Quill Design is a registered trademark of Harcourt Brace & Company.

Acknowledgments appear in the back of this work.

Printed in the United States of America

ISBN 0-15-310628-X

5 6 7 8 9 10   048   2000 99

Dear Reader,

You'll find that the families of animals and people in this book have big wishes and dreams. They are a lot like you. Read the stories. Enjoy the poems. Meet all kinds of families like yours. **Big Dreams** can come from reading. So open up the book and follow your dreams.

Sincerely,

The Authors

The Authors

All in a Family

Special family times—which ones are the best? Share some fun with families as you read these stories.

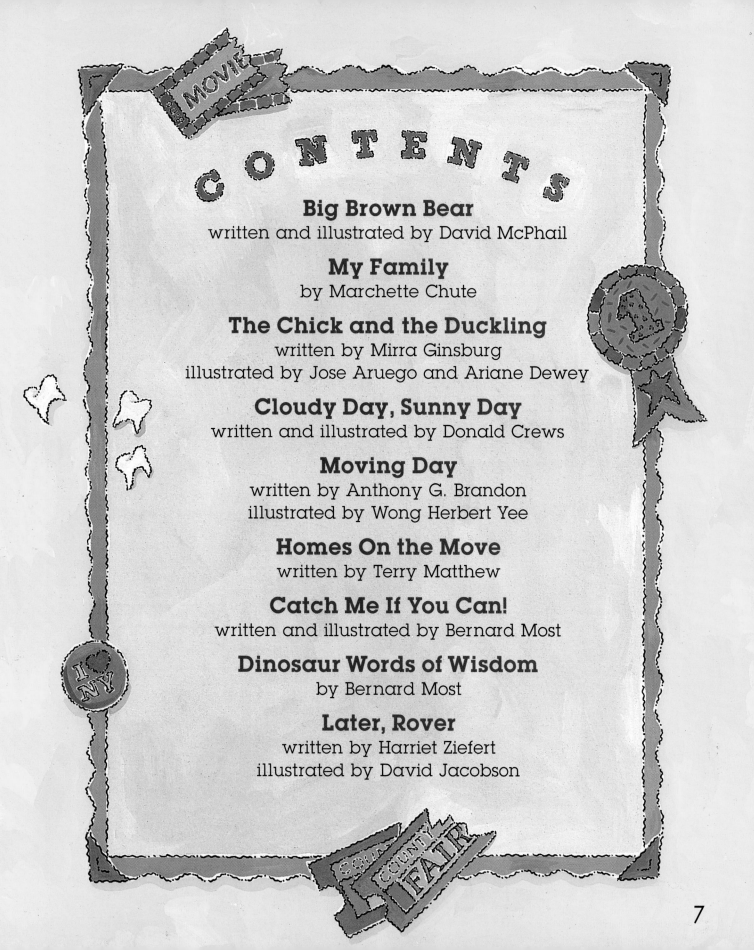

CONTENTS

BOOKSHELF

Five Little Monkeys Jumping on the Bed

by Eileen Christelow

Five little monkeys think bedtime is playtime.

Children's Choice

SIGNATURES LIBRARY

Vegetable Garden

by Douglas Florian

What kinds of seeds will a family plant to make their garden grow?

Outstanding Science Trade Book for Children

SIGNATURES LIBRARY

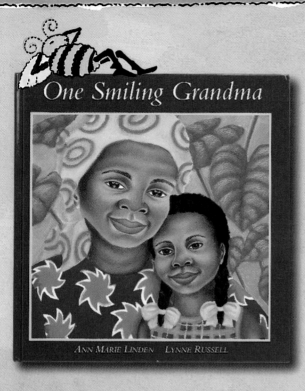

One Smiling Grandma

by Ann Marie Linden

A girl finds many reasons to smile with her grandmother.

Hide and Seek in the Yellow House

by Agatha Rose

Will Mother Cat ever find where her kitten, Mack, is hiding?

Big Brown Bear

by David McPhail

BIG BOOK

Award-Winning
Author/Illustrator

Big
Brown
Bear

written and illustrated
by David McPhail

Bear is big.

Bear is brown.

Bear goes up.

He comes down.

Bear gets paint.
The paint is blue.

Bear goes up.
The paint goes, too.

Little Bear is playing.
She has a bat.

Oh, no! Little Bear!
Do not do that!

Bear was up.
Bear comes down.

Bear is big. . .
But he's not brown!

Bear washes up.
He's brown once more.

He washes the windows,
then the door.

Bear gets more paint.
It's green, not blue.

Bear goes up.
The paint goes, too.

Bear is painting.
He's all set.

But look out, Bear!

It's not over yet!

David McPhail

Many of David McPhail's books have bears in them. He likes to draw bears. They remind him of Teddy, the bear he had when he was little. Teddy would go with him everywhere.

David McPhail doesn't have Teddy anymore, but he has another big toy bear in his office that keeps him company. Who keeps you company?

David McPhail

My Family

by Marchette Chute

Part of my family is grown-up and tall.
Part of my family is little and small.
I'm in the middle and pleased with
 them all.

A Beary Nice

In the story, Bear went up and Bear went down. Sing this song about something else Bear might do!

The bear went over the mountain.
The bear went over the mountain.
The bear went over the mountain—
To see what he could see!

32

Sing-Along!

To see what he could see!
To see what he could see!
The bear went over the mountain—
To see what he could see!

34

The Chick
and the Duckling
Translated from the Russian of V. Suteyev
by Mirra Ginsburg
Pictures by Jose Aruego & Ariane Dewey

The Chick

and the

Duckling

by Mirra Ginsburg

pictures by Jose Aruego and Ariane Dewey

translated from the Russian of V. Suteyev

Award-
Winning Author

Award-Winning
Illustrators

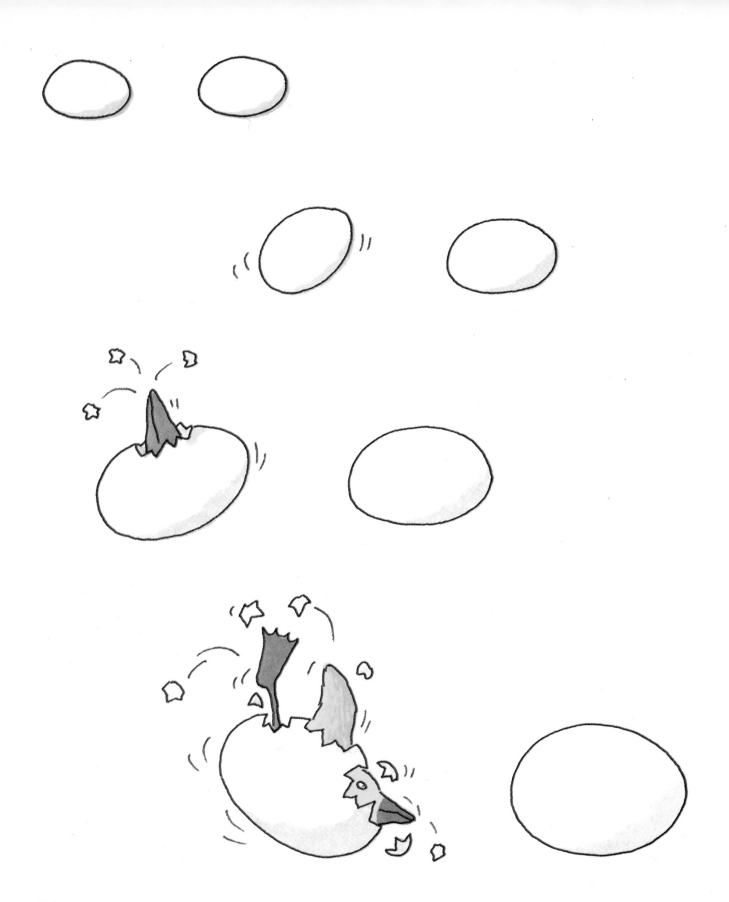

A Duckling came out
of the shell.

"I am out!" he said.

38

"Me too," said the Chick.

"I am taking a walk,"
said the Duckling.

"Me too,"
said the Chick.

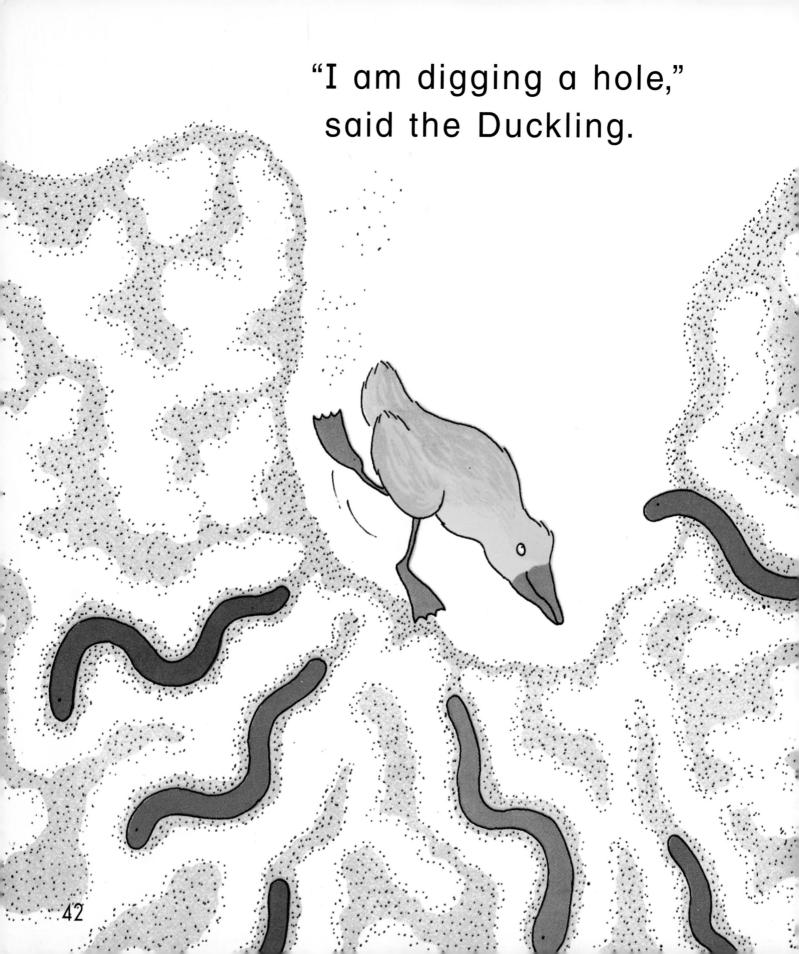

"I am digging a hole,"
said the Duckling.

42

"Me too,"
said the Chick.

"I found a worm,"
said the Duckling.

"Me too,"
said the Chick.

"I caught
a butterfly,"
said the
Duckling.

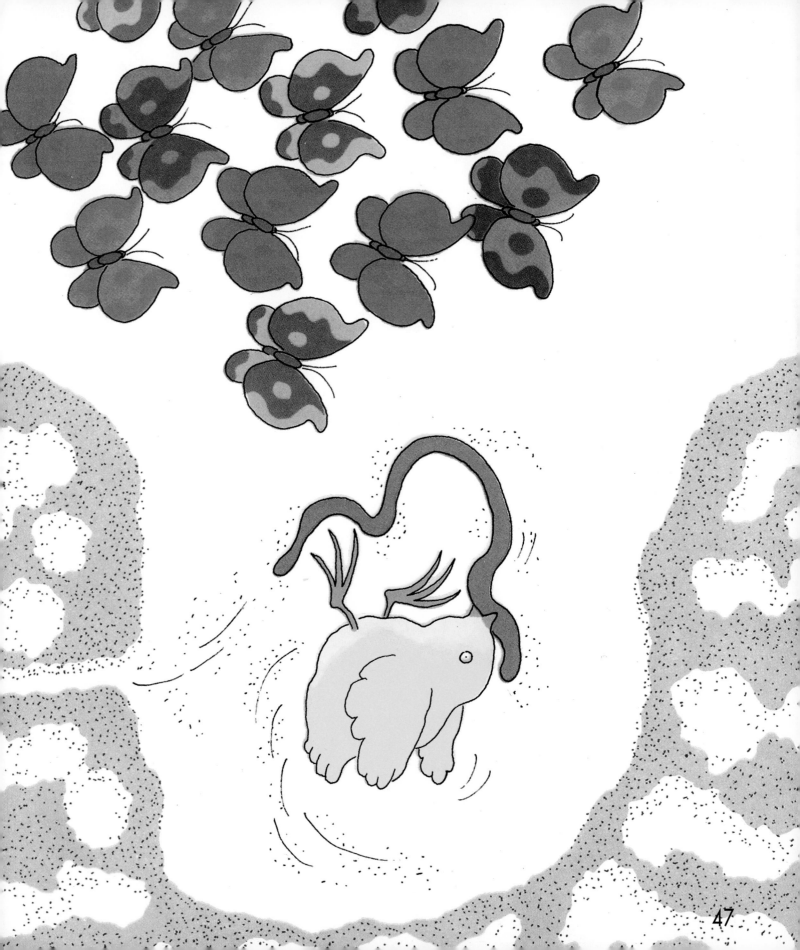

"Me too,"
said the Chick.

49

"I am going for a swim,"
said the Duckling.

"Me too,"
said the Chick.

51

"I am swimming,"
said the Duckling.

"Me too!"
cried the Chick.

The Duckling pulled
the Chick out.

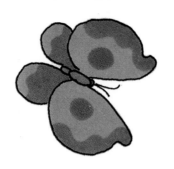

"I'm going for another swim,"
said the Duckling.

"Not me,"
said the Chick.

Mirra Ginsburg

Mirra Ginsburg grew up in Russia, where she saw lots of animals. They were in the woods, on farms, and in courtyards. *The Chick and the Duckling* is a Russian story that she wanted to tell in English.

Jose Aruego and Ariane Dewey

Jose Aruego grew up in the Philippines. His family had many animals—horses, dogs, cats, chickens, ducks, and pigs. His books always have funny animals doing funny things.

Ariane Dewey and Jose Aruego have worked as a team to illustrate many children's books.

61

I Can Do

The Chick and the Duckling did many things together. Make a book to show what special things you can do with your family and friends.

 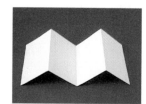 Fold a big sheet of paper to make an accordion book.

 Make a cover.

  Draw pictures of things you can do with your family and friends.

This!

Share your book with a group.

63

Cloudy Day Sunny Day

words and pictures by

Donald Crews

BIG BOOK

Award-Winning
Author/Illustrator

Words and Pictures by Donald Crews

Cloudy
Day
Sunny
Day

It's a cloudy day.

A gray day.

A gray, cloudy,
and gloomy day.

A day to stay in and play.

A day for reading books.

A day for make-believe.

A day for drawing and painting.

71

We have lots of fun
on gray, cloudy, gloomy days.

LOOK! THE SUN! THE SUN!

THE SUN'S OUT!

74

Let's go out.
Let's go out and play.

It's a sunny day.

A running, jumping day.

It's a sunny day.

A day to throw and catch.

A day to scream and shout.

It's a sunny day.
A day to fly a kite.

It's a sunny day.
A day to ride a bike.

**Cloudy days, sunny days,
fun days.**

Meet Donald

Dear Readers,

On cloudy days, I enjoy reading, writing, drawing, and building model airplanes. On sunny days, I like to take a walk outside and look at everything that is going on around me.

What do you enjoy doing on a cloudy or sunny day? Enjoy the things you do. Also, find something that you're good at and stick with it.

Your friend,

Crews

HERE COMES THE SUN

What do you do when the sun is out?
Make a class mural to show "sunny day" fun.

86

mural paper

paints

brushes

1 Paint a picture to show what *you* do when the sun is out.

2 Then tell the group about your part of the mural.

Is today a sunny day? Choose something fun from the mural to do outdoors.

Moving Day

written by Anthony G. Brandon

illustrated by Wong Herbert Yee

On moving day, Mr. and Mrs. Kim were moving.

Jenny Kim was moving.
Jack Kim was moving.

But not Annie.

"I'm not going," said Annie.
She sat on a box.

"Let's go," said Mrs. Kim.
"I'm not going," said Annie.

"You have to go," said Jenny.
"I'm not going," said Annie.

"We all have to go," said Jack.
"Well, I'm not going," said Annie.

"You will have a big yard,"
said Mrs. Kim.

"I like my little yard!" said Annie.

"You will have a big room,"
said Mr. Kim.

"I like my little room!" said Annie.

"You will make new friends,"
said Jenny.

"I like my old friends," said Annie.

It was time to go.

"Annie, pick up the last box," said Mrs. Kim.
"I'll get it, but I'm still not going," said Annie.

"Is this puppy going?"

"Yes," they all said.
"Well, then I'm going too!"

Wong Herbert Yee

Where do you get ideas for your stories?

I think about lots of things. I think about everything around me. I think about myself as a little boy and about my daughter when she was a first grader.

What is your favorite thing to draw?

I like drawing animals—especially animals wearing clothes! The rabbit in "Moving Day" is special to me because it is my daughter's favorite stuffed animal. I like to put this rabbit in every story I do.

Wong Herbert Yee

Pack Your Suitcase

Pretend it is your moving day. What special things will you pack? Make a suitcase for your things.

You will need:

construction paper

pipe cleaners

crayons

magazines

scissors

glue

hole punch

1. Fold the paper in half.

2. Make a handle for each side.

3. Fill your suitcase with pictures.

Ask a friend to guess what is in your suitcase.
Then **show** and **tell** what you have.

Homes On

Some homes are easy to move. Can you see why? People can live in homes like these. Why might it be a good idea to move a home easily?

American Indian tepees

the Move

Central Asian yurts

Tent

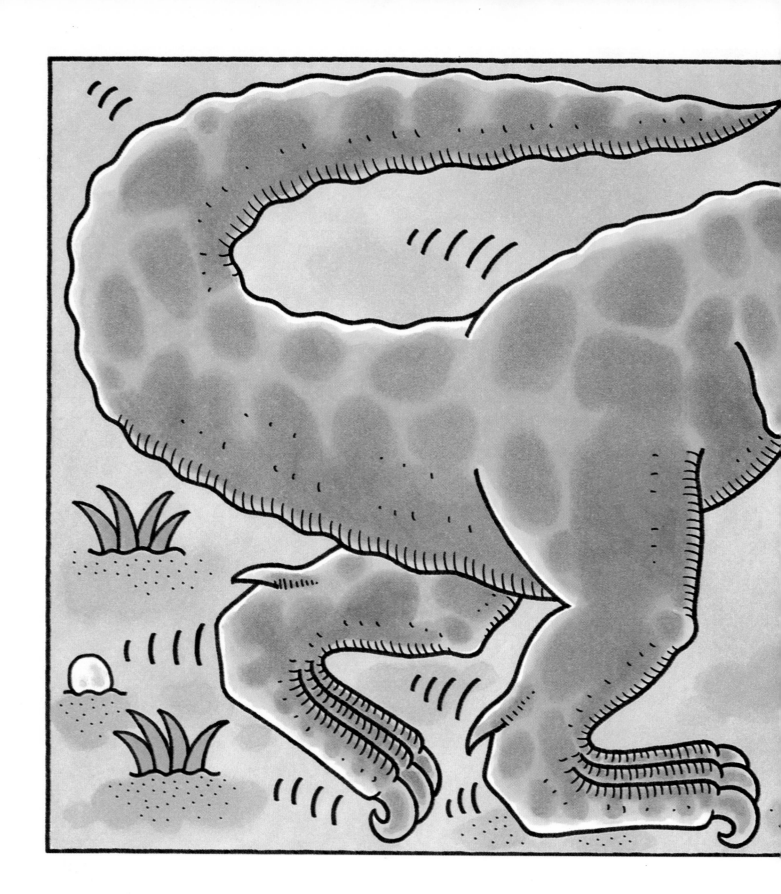

BIG BOOK

Award-Winning
Author/Illustrator

Catch Me
If You Can!

written and illustrated
by Bernard Most

He was the biggest dinosaur of
them all. The other dinosaurs were
afraid of him.

When the biggest dinosaur went by,
the other dinosaurs quickly hid.

They were afraid of his
great big tail.

They were afraid of his
great big claws.

They were afraid of his
great big feet.

But most of all, they were afraid
of his great big teeth.

One little dinosaur wasn't afraid.
She didn't run. She didn't hide.

"Catch me if you can!" she called
to the biggest dinosaur.

"I'm not afraid of your
great big tail."

"Catch me if you can!"

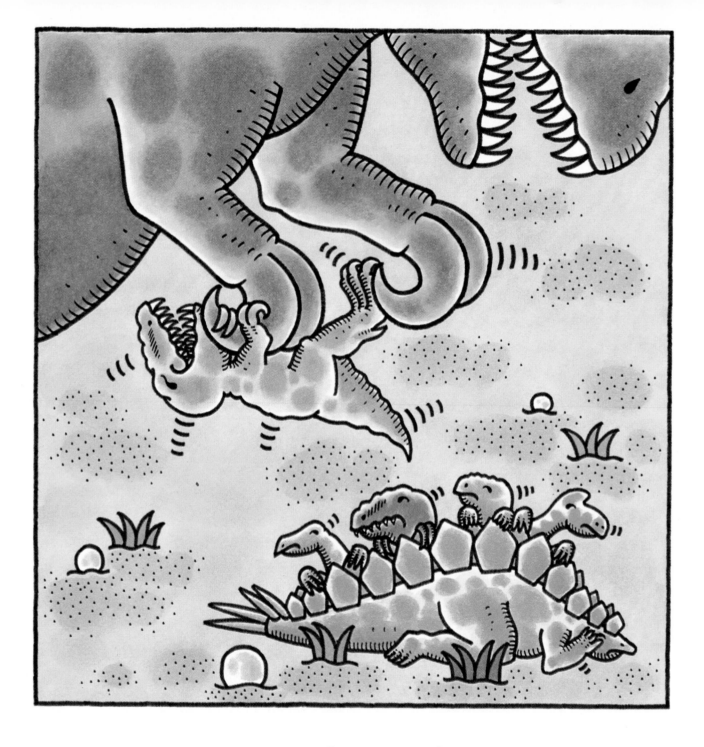

"I'm not afraid of your
great big claws."

"Catch me if you can!"

"I'm not afraid of your
great big feet."

"Catch me if you can!"

"And most of all, I'm not afraid
of your great big teeth."

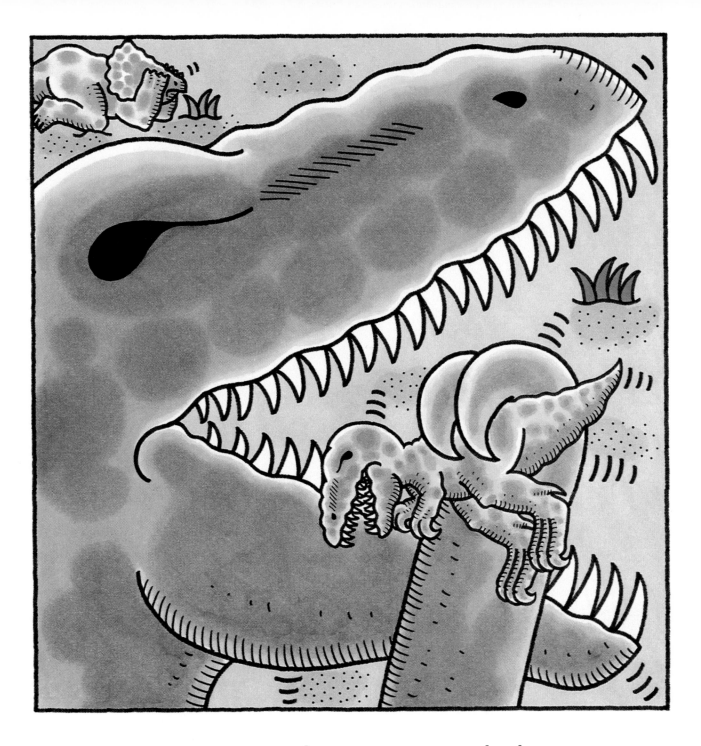

"I can catch you!" said the
biggest dinosaur. And he
grabbed the little dinosaur.

But she only got a big hug.
"I love you very much, Grandpa!"
said the little dinosaur.

"And I love you, too!" said the
biggest dinosaur of them all.

Bernard Most

Bernard Most knew he wanted to be an artist even before he went to kindergarten. Later, he went to art school and became an artist. He saw some books by Leo Lionni and liked them so much that he started to write his own books for children.

Bernard Most works hard on his books. He sent out one book 42 times before it was published! He didn't give up. He knows how important it is to believe in yourself and to keep trying.

Bernard Most

DINOSAUR
Words of Wisdom

●●●●●●●●●●●●●●●●●●●

by Bernard Most

Go to bed late,
Stay very small.
Go to bed early,
Grow very tall.

DINOSAUR TAG

Play a dinosaur game with a big group of children.

1. Line up. Put your hands 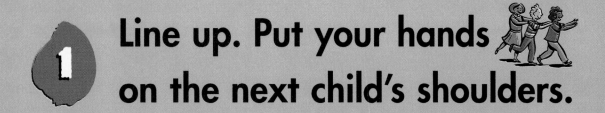 on the next child's shoulders.

2. The first child is the head. The last child is the tail.

3. The head tries to catch the tail.

If the head catches the tail, play again!
If the line breaks, the head goes to the tail. Then play again.

LATER, ROVER

Harriet Ziefert • Pictures by David Jacobson

Later, Rover

Award-Winning Author

written by Harriet Ziefert
pictures by David Jacobson

"Hello, Dad," Andy said.
"Will you play with me?"

"Later, Andy," said Dad.

"Hello, Mom," Andy said.
"Will you play with me?"

"Later, Andy," said Mom.

"Hello, Dad," Andy said.
"Now will you play?"

"Later, Andy," said Dad.

"Hello, Mom," Andy said.
"Now will you play?"

"Later, Andy," said Mom.

"There is a monster in the garden.
It's going to eat me!" said Andy.

"Later, Andy," said Dad.

"There is a robot in the hall.
He wants to speak to you!"
said Andy.

"Later, Andy," said Mom.

"Hi, Amy," Andy said.
"Mom and Dad are busy.
Will you play with me?"

"Later, Andy," said Amy.

Andy went outside.
He sat by himself.

Then he called Rover.
"Here, Rover," yelled Andy.
"Come here!"

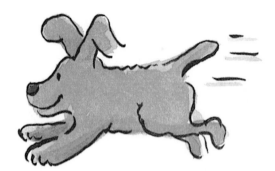

Rover came.

He sniffed.

He wagged his tail.

"Will you play with me?"
Andy asked.

"Arf! Arf!" barked Rover.

Andy threw a stick.
Rover ran to get it.

"Good dog!"
Andy said.

159

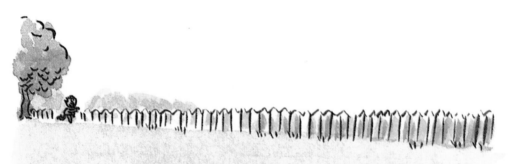

Andy threw the stick again.

Rover caught it.
"Good catch!" Andy said.

Andy threw the stick
again and again.

Rover caught it
again and again.
"Good game!" Andy said.

Then Andy got tired.

"Last throw," he said to Rover.

"Not now," said Andy.
"Later, Rover!"

Harriet Ziefert

Harriet Ziefert taught elementary school for many years. She has written many, many books. She writes quickly. It takes her about twelve hours to write each one. After that, she works with an artist to create illustrations for it. Then she changes some of the words until the story is just right.

Good Game!

Everyone was too busy to play with Andy, except Rover. You can play this game with Rover, too!

Draw a big picture of Rover with lots of spots.

Take turns rolling the number cube.

Put that many counters on Rover's spots.
You and your partner use different color counters.

Play until all spots are covered.

The player with more counters on Rover wins!

You will need:

 big sheet of paper

 crayons or markers

number cube

 counters, 2 colors

After you play:

Write down the rules for a new game using your Rover game board.

· · · · · · · · · · · · · · · · ⁛ · · · · · · · · · · · · · · · ·

Teach a friend how to play it.

Acknowledgments

For permission to reprint copyrighted material, grateful acknowledgment is made to the following sources:

Dutton Children's Books, a division of Penguin Books USA Inc.: Cover illustration from *Fix-It* by David McPhail. Copyright © 1984 by David McPhail.

Greenwillow Books, a division of William Morrow & Company, Inc.: Cover illustration from *Sail Away* by Donald Crews. Copyright © 1995 by Donald Crews. Cover illustration from *School Bus* by Donald Crews. Copyright © 1984 by Donald Crews. Cover illustration from *Flying* by Donald Crews. Copyright © 1986 by Donald Crews. Cover illustration by Jose Aruego and Ariane Dewey from *Merry-Go-Round: Four Stories* by Mirra Ginsburg. Illustration copyright © 1977, 1981, 1992 by Jose Aruego and Ariane Dewey. Cover illustration by Byron Barton from *Good Morning, Chick* by Mirra Ginsburg. Illustration copyright © 1980 by Byron Barton.

Harcourt Brace & Company: Cover illustration from *The Littlest Dinosaurs* by Bernard Most. Copyright © 1989 by Bernard Most. Cover illustration from *Where to Look for a Dinosaur* by Bernard Most. Copyright © 1993 by Bernard Most. Cover illustration from *How Big Were the Dinosaurs?* by Bernard Most. Copyright © 1994 by Bernard Most.

HarperCollins Publishers: From *Four & Twenty Dinosaurs* (Retitled: "Dinosaur Words of Wisdom") by Bernard Most. Copyright © 1990 by Bernard Most.

Houghton Mifflin Company: Cover illustration from *Mrs. Brown Went to Town* by Wong Herbert Yee. Copyright © 1996 by Wong Herbert Yee. Cover illustration from *EEK! There's a Mouse in the House* by Wong Herbert Yee. Copyright © 1992 by Wong Herbert Yee. Cover illustration from *Fireman Small* by Wong Herbert Yee. Copyright © 1994 by Wong Herbert Yee. Cover illustration from *Big Black Bear* by Wong Herbert Yee. Copyright © 1993 by Wong Herbert Yee.

Alfred A. Knopf, Inc.: Cover illustration by Anita Lobel from *A New Coat for Anna* by Harriet Ziefert. Illustration copyright © 1986 by Anita Lobel.

Little, Brown and Company: Cover illustration from *Edward and the Pirates* by David McPhail. Copyright © 1997 by David McPhail.

Puffin Books, a division of Penguin Books USA Inc.: Later, Rover by Harriet Ziefert, illustrated by David Jacobson. Text copyright © 1991 by Harriet Ziefert; illustrations copyright © 1991 by David Jacobson.

Elizabeth M. Roach: "My Family" from *Rhymes About Us* by Marchette Chute. Text copyright 1974 by Marchette Chute. Published by E. P. Dutton.

Random House, Inc.: Cover illustration by Andrea Baruffi from *The Wheels on the Bus* by Harriet Ziefert. Illustration copyright © 1990 by Andrea Baruffi.

Scholastic Inc.: Cover illustration from *The Day the Dog Said, "Cock-a-Doodle-Doo!"* by David McPhail. Copyright © 1997 by David McPhail. Published by CARTWHEEL BOOKS. CARTWHEEL BOOKS and HELLO READER! are registered trademarks of Scholastic Inc.

Simon & Schuster Books for Young Readers, Simon & Schuster Children's Publishing Division: The Chick and the Duckling, translated from the Russian of V. Suteyev by Mirra Ginsburg, illustrated by Jose and Ariane Aruego. Text copyright © 1972 by Mirra Ginsburg; illustrations copyright © 1972 by Jose Aruego. Cover illustration by Jose Aruego and Ariane Dewey from *Herman the Helper* by Robert Kraus. Illustration copyright © 1974 by Jose Aruego and Ariane Dewey.

Viking Penguin, a division of Penguin Books USA Inc.: Cover illustration by Mavis Smith from *Let's Get a Pet* by Harriet Ziefert. Illustration copyright © 1993 by Mavis Smith.

Photo Credits
Key: (t)=top, (b)=bottom, (c)=center, (l)=left, (r)=right.

Pages 32, 33, 62, 63, 86, 87, 110, 111, 138, 139, 166, 167, Campos Photography. Page 4-5, Weronica Ankarorn/Harcourt Brace & Company; 29, Rick Friedman / Black Star / Harcourt Brace & Co.; 62(t), courtesy, Macmillan; 62(b), Walt Chrynwski / Black Star / Harcourt Brace & Co.; 85, Alan Orling / Black Star / Harcourt Brace & Co.; 109, Santa Fabio / Black Star / Harcourt Brace & Co.; 112, Lawrence Migdale; 112-113, Bachmann / Photo Researchers; 113(t), Photo Researchers; 113(b), Ken Cole / Earth Scenes; 135, Walt Chrynwski / Black Star / Harcourt Brace & Co.

Illustration Credits
Doug Bowles, Cover art; Brenda York, 4-9; David McPhail, 10-29; Jose Aruego & Ariane Dewey, 34-61; Donald Crews, 64-85; Wong Herbert Yee, 88-109; Bernard Most, 114-135, 136-137; David Jacobson, 140-165